Machines at Work

Tanks

by Allan Morey

Bullfrog Books

Ideas for Parents and Teachers

Bullfrog Books let children practice reading informational text at the earliest reading levels. Repetition, familiar words, and photo labels support early readers.

Before Reading

- Discuss the cover photo. What does it tell them?

- Look at the picture glossary together. Read and discuss the words.

Read the Book

- "Walk" through the book and look at the photos. Let the child ask questions. Point out the photo labels.

- Read the book to the child, or have him or her read independently.

After Reading

- Prompt the child to think more. Ask: Have you ever seen a tank? Was it driving around?

Bullfrog Books are published by Jump!
5357 Penn Avenue South
Minneapolis, MN 55419
www.jumplibrary.com

Library of Congress Cataloging-in-Publication Data

Morey, Allan.
  Tanks / by Allan Morey.
    pages cm. — (Machines at work)
  Includes bibliographical references and index.
  Summary: "This photo-illustrated book for early readers explains the parts of tanks that help keep the crew safe when they go into battle" — Provided by publisher.
  Audience: Grades K-3.
  ISBN 978-1-62031-106-6 (hard cover) —
  ISBN 978-1-62496-175-5 (ebook)
  1. Tanks (Military science) — Juvenile literature.
I. Title.
  UG446.5.M587 2014
  623.74'752—dc23
                                      2013047819

Series Editor: Wendy Dieker
Series Designer: Ellen Huber
Book Designer: Anna Peterson
Photo Researcher: Kurtis Kinneman

Photo Credits: Alamy/ARCTIC IMAGES, 14–15, 23bl; Alamy/Caro, 19 (inset); Alamy/Stephen Barnes/Military, 14 (inset); Defense Imagery/Master Sgt. Reeba Critser, 9; Dreamstime/Stangot, 17; iStock/belterz, 12–13, 23tl; Shutterstock/-= PHANTOM =-, 3; Shutterstock/1125089601, 6–7; Shutterstock/Creativa, 1; Shutterstock/Degtyaryov Andrey, 4; Shutterstock/itakefotos4u, 10–11; Shutterstock/Len Green, 22; Shutterstock/makarenko7, 8; Shutterstock/risteski goce, cover; Shutterstock/S-F, 16, 23tr; Shutterstock/slavapolo, 10 (inset), 23br; Shutterstock/Studio 37, 5; Shutterstock/yuri4u80, 24; Toshi12/Dreamstime.com, 20–21; U.S. Department of Defense / Science Faction/SuperStock, 18–19

Printed in the United States of America at Corporate Graphics, in North Mankato, Minnesota.
3-2014
10 9 8 7 6 5 4 3 2 1

Table of Contents

Tanks at Work

Look at the dust!

A tank is going to war.

machine gun

Jim aims the machine gun.

He shoots at close targets.

The big gun shoots far away.

Boom!

9

Look at the mud!

The tank has tracks.

It moves.

It does not get stuck.

tracks

Do you see the armor?

It covers the tank.

It keeps the
crew safe.

armor

The crew rides in the tank.

Al is the driver.

He steers.

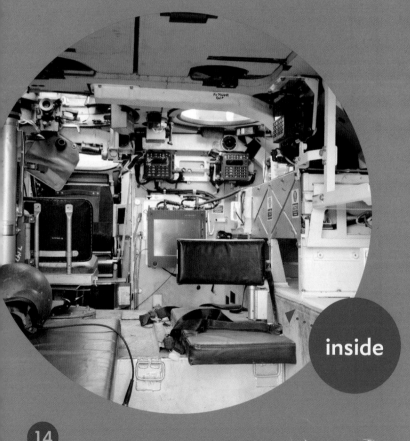

inside

driver

Sue is the gunner.

She aims the big gun.

The top of the tank spins around.

There is the target.
Fire! Boom!
It is a hit!

The battle is won!

Parts of a Tank

machine gun
The machine gun shoots small bullets.

hatch
The hole where soldiers get in and out of a tank.

main gun
The cannon shoots large shells.

turret
The top part of a tank where the main gun is located.

Picture Glossary

armor
The metal plates that cover the outside of a tank to protect the soldiers inside.

gunner
A member of a tank crew who aims and fires the main gun.

crew
A group of soldiers who work together in a tank.

tracks
Wide, heavy metal links around the tank's wheels that help it drive over mud.

Index

To Learn More

Learning more is as easy as 1, 2, 3.

1) Go to www.factsurfer.com

2) Enter "tank" into the search box.

3) Click the "Surf" button to see a list of websites.

With factsurfer.com, finding more information is just a click away.